Preaching To Myself

And Other Hints On How To Preach Great Sermons 52 Weeks A Year

Barbara G. Schmitz

CSS Publishing Company, Inc., Lima, Ohio

PREACHING TO MYSELF

Copyright © 2002 by
CSS Publishing Company, Inc.
Lima, Ohio

Library of Congress Cataloging-in-Publication Data

Schmitz, Barbara G., 1958-
    Preaching to myself : and other hints on how to preach great sermons 52 weeks a year
/ Barbara G. Schmitz.
        p. cm.
Includes bibliographical references.
    ISBN 0-7880-1945-7 (pbk. : alk. paper)
    1. Preaching. I. Title.
    BV4211.3 S36 2003
    251—dc21

                                                                            2002013719

For more information about CSS Publishing Company resources, visit our website at
www.csspub.com or e-mail us at custserv@csspub.com or call (800) 241-4056.

ISBN 0-7880-1945-7
PRINTED IN U.S.A.

*In memory of my
Uncle Bob, who always
enjoyed telling
a good story*

Acknowledgements

My thanks to Bonnie and Brenda for their prophetic voices which birthed this book; the faithful parishioners at the parishes where I have served, for their wholehearted response to my preaching; and my parents and long-time friends, Sharon, Joan, and Sharon, for their encouragement and support.

The sources for several stories could not be found. I would be glad to include proper acknowledgements in any future editions. Please contact the publisher with information.

Table Of Contents

Preface

Why another book on preaching?

The story goes that one day, a young preacher was discouraged because he wasn't seeing any results from his preaching. The great preacher Phillips Brooks asked him, "Son, you don't expect to see repentance, conversion, and changed parishioners every time you preach, do you?" The young man replied, "No, sir." Brooks thought for a moment and then answered, "That's your problem."

I agree with Phillips Brooks. We preachers often do not have enough holy expectation. There were times in the past when that was true of me. But now I live to preach. God gives me a sermon every week, and I've got to preach it. Sometimes I say something like this to the congregation: "I didn't get up at 5 a.m. to be on the road at 6 a.m. Sunday morning to come preach here for nothing. I didn't grope in the dark to pull on my pantyhose and get ready to go to church for nothing. Listen; if 'nothing' is going to happen as a result of the sermon, then I'd rather stay at home. If nothing is going to happen, then I'll sleep in, stay in my pajamas, put on a pot of coffee, read the Sunday newspaper, watch the Sunday morning political commentary shows, and snuggle with the cats. I didn't get up before dawn because you have great coffee here. I got up and came because I am expecting God to speak to us and do something this morning."

I can't put this holy expectation deep down inside of you, but I can explain the practical side of crafting a sermon, as various folks over the years have asked me to do. This primer on preaching is offered as the most down-to-earth, practical instruction manual you may ever read on how to preach in the trenches of everyday life for real people. It is everything I know about how to write great sermons that impact and change lives every time you preach, 52 weeks a year.

Barbara G. Schmitz
Pentecost 2002
Saginaw, Michigan

one

Nuts And Bolts

1. Everything Is Fodder

Where does the stuff of sermons come from? The stuff of sermons comes from everyday living. Everything is fodder. Every book you read, every person you talk to, every prayer you pray, every movie you see, every newspaper you read, every walk you take, every dream you dream — all is fodder. The first key is recognizing that you have sermon material. The second key is capturing it so that you have a record of it. The third key is accessing it, so that two years from now, when you've long forgotten about it, you are able to retrieve it at precisely the moment you need it.

2. A Story A Day

First comes the ability to recognize good sermon material. That's not too hard to do. Either something deeply moves you, or the light simply goes on in your head — this would be a great story for a sermon (someday), or you instantly recognize that this is spiritual stuff and it would make a great sermon story. Basically, any event or story that moves you is probably ripe material for a sermon. The problem is not having enough stories; it's having too many stories. Let's say for now that just one thing per day occurs that will be useful somewhere, somehow, in a future sermon. You don't even have to know exactly how it might be used; you just know it's a good story. Let's focus on recognizing that one item each day.

One of my favorite places to get sermons is bumper stickers. Bumper stickers make for good sermon texts, titles, and outlines.

One I saw recently said, "Get in, sit down, buckle up, be alert." Might make for a good sermon on discipleship or joining the church.

3. Taking Notes

Perhaps the single most important activity that separates good preachers from great preachers is the willingness to take time to make notes. This may well be the hardest part. It takes dedication, even sacrifice, and this may be what separates the good preachers from the great preachers: the willingness to take the time *now* to make a note which will be used in a future sermon a month, a year, or a decade from now. I have pulled off the side of the road to write down a line from a song that I wanted to remember and use. I have gotten out of bed to make notes after waking up from a dream. I have photocopied pages of a book that had a story I knew would make a good sermon illustration some day. Capturing good sermon material just means making the time to capture the story now.

4. Setting Up A Good Retrieval System

It is wonderful to have great stories and good notes, but you've also got to file them in such a way that you will find them precisely when you need them. This sounds harder than it is. It simply takes a good filing and retrieval system. The one I recommend and use is a filing system that may take a little more time upfront to file the story in the right place, but the payoff is instant and painless retrieval.

I have three sets of files. The first, and largest, is a file of the key passages in scripture, in the same order as the books of the Bible. So my files start with Genesis 1, Genesis 2, and go through Revelation. The Gospels of Matthew, Mark, and Luke, however, are set up slightly differently. My Gospel files are not in the order: Matthew, Mark, and Luke. Rather, they are set up by "parallel" so that, for example, the parallel passages of Jesus' baptism (found in Matthew, Mark, and Luke) are all in one file (#6), the parallel passages of Jesus' temptation are in the next file (#7, 8), and so on. To set up and number your files in this manner, all you need to do is buy a parallel of the Gospel (Burton H. Throckmorton, Jr.'s is the one I use), and label and set up your files using the parallel number system. Note that Throckmorton begins his numbering with the birth of John the Baptist, so the infancy narratives need their own numbering system. You can use a, b, c, etc. or simply file them by subject (the Magnificat, the Magi, etc.). Likewise, the resurrection appearances at the end of the three Gospels are not numbered.

The second set of files is by theme, filed alphabetically, and includes titles that I preach on most often, such as: Church, Discipleship, Faith, Forgiveness, God, Healing, Heaven, Holy Spirit, Hope, Love, Miracles, Money, Peace, Praise, Reconciliation, Sin. You'll have your own titles.

The third set is a liturgical set that parallels the church year. So I have a set of files titled Advent, Epiphany, Lent, Good Friday, Easter, Pentecost, Trinity Sunday, etc. Depending on your denomination, you may not want or need a set like this.

If you have all three sets of files in place and ready to go, then the next task is probably the hardest. It is deciding where to file this little nugget of a potential sermon item that you have captured. If the item naturally suggests a scripture passage, file it there. If you are like me, it may take you a little research to find the book, chapter, and verse of the passage using a concordance. If it is a Matthew/Mark/Luke scripture, you may have to work to find the parallel number for that passage (hang in there — filing items this way does take some getting used to).

If the item doesn't naturally suggest a place to file it, you have to do a little thinking. Okay, so it's a great item. Think about the context in which you might possibly use it. Is it an Easter story? A story that would go well with a sermon on healing? Is there any passage in scripture to which you can imagine this relating? Give it your best shot and file it there. If you're still stumped, here are two back-ups: First, create one more file called "great stories" and file your item in there for temporary storage. Maybe later you'll think of exactly where that item should be filed. In the meantime, if you are absolutely stuck some week and can't think of anything to preach, you can always pull out your "great stories" file and see what's in there. The second back-up is, don't worry; if you file it in the "wrong" file, you'll come across it in the future as you are preparing another sermon, and you can file it in a better place then.

The point is, just get it in the best file you can now. Again, this is the hard part, but your labor will be amply rewarded later.

Over time, your files will build nicely. Imagine what joy it will be a year or two or ten from now when you pull a file to preach a sermon, and find a ready stock of sermon ideas!

By the way, this is also where you will file your preached sermons, so over time you will also be building a file of all the sermons you've preached on this scripture/subject/liturgical season. Just like the stories you file, file your sermons according to the primary scripture passage, subject, or liturgical season to which they relate.

5. I Know I Preached That About A Year Ago ...

Two housekeeping matters that will greatly help: First, jot on your sermon outline or notes the following information each time you preach: the title, the liturgical day (e.g. first Sunday of Lent, Easter, Reformation Sunday, etc.), the main scripture passage used in the sermon, and the date and the place where you preached it.

Then do this to keep track of all your sermons. On a one-page sheet that you organize on a computer spreadsheet, record the date, the liturgical day, the main scripture text, the church (especially if you preach at various churches), the title of the sermon, and most importantly, where you will file it.

Keeping track of all sermons in this way has saved me many times from pulling out my hair trying to find a sermon in the files. Often I am looking for a particular sermon and I'll vaguely remember when I preached it or where, but I won't necessarily remember where I filed it. This "cheat sheet" comes in particularly useful when I will be preaching at a church and want to make sure that I don't tell them the same stories I used the last time I was there. I can quickly pull a record of the sermons I've preached at that church, look up the files, and see what stories I used. I don't worry it if it's been a couple of years or more since generally people don't remember even the very best stories I use, but on major feast days, such as Easter or Christmas, I don't want to repeat the same sermon.

two

Crafting A Sermon

1. Praying Monday Night

Often, if the sermon goes well, I come home Sunday afternoon all excited to start working on next Sunday's sermon immediately. At this point I impose a Sabbath rest. I have made it my practice not to think about the next Sunday's sermon until at least Monday evening. This gives a good solid break. As a Sabbath rest from sermon writing, it reminds me that my sermons are a God thing, and that I depend on God. At least one evening, and a continuous stretch off from doing anything with a sermon, will provide a good rebound and Sabbath time.

Usually on Monday evening I sit down to begin work on my next sermon. As a preacher in a church that uses a lectionary (appointed texts for each Sunday), the decision about what scriptures to use is already decided for me. But I do not look at the appointed scripture texts. Instead, I designate Monday evening as a time of preparation and prayer. I started doing this a few years ago when I began preaching in different churches every Sunday. Preaching in a different church every Sunday at first was very awkward, since I often did not know anyone but the person who called to arrange my coming to preach, and the treasurer who handed me a check for the service. How could I preach a sermon to people I didn't know? I would really have to seek God's heart for what I was supposed to preach. So that's when I started my sermon preparation on Monday night by praying. There was no other possible, conceivable way to have any assurance that I was preaching what they needed to hear, than to ask God. So this is basically my prayer: "God, show me what they need to hear this Sunday. Put your message for them on my heart. Direct me to the particular aspect of these scriptures that they need." So now, even though I may be preaching to a group I do know, this is still how I start my sermon preparation — by praying.

2. Percolating

I think the best sermons are sermons that percolate over the course of the week. It is usually Tuesday morning when I sit down to look at the appointed lessons for the first time. This is like grinding up coffee beans and putting them in the filter basket, and turning the coffee machine on. It's the raw material, step one. Then all during the week, my thoughts, my experiences, conversations, books, world events — are going to run through the scriptures like water through the coffee grounds. It is this percolating process that brings out the richness of the beans, and through the week my life will filter down through those scriptures and bring out their full flavor. It's a process of time. It's not a mental exercise I sit down to on Saturday night. A sermon is something I have lived with all week.

Part of the necessary percolating process for preachers is studying the appointed texts (or, in traditions without a lectionary, the scripture passages you have chosen). I assume you have text study resources and know how to use them. It is also great if you can be part of a text study group with other pastors. As you hone in on exactly what scripture passages you'll be using, doing the exegetical work is great preparation.

Another part of the percolating process is pulling the three or so most related files. As a preacher in a church that uses a set lectionary (appointed scripture readings for each Sunday), I usually pull the files for each appointed scripture, and at least one file from my subject file and/or seasonal file. As time goes on, these files are thicker and thicker, chock full of stories, possible themes, ideas, quotes, etc. Since old sermons are filed in there, I can also refresh my memory with what I have preached in the past and also avoid preaching the same sermon twice to the same group of people.

3. Drafting

Generally I start writing up the first draft of the sermon on Saturday morning. By that time, I usually have some thoughts in my head or on paper based on the percolating process through the week — some preliminary things that struck me, a story from my files that I thought might go well with one of the scripture texts, an experience that seems related, etc. I sit down with a yellow legal pad and write down, if I haven't already, all the things I can possibly think of that are related to one or more of the lessons. It is important not internally to "edit" this list in my head — I write down every thought I've had, whether it seems to be a piece I can use in my sermon or not. I stay away from trying to order, or sequence, the material until later.

Occasionally this list is very short and you know you are in big trouble! This may be a sign that you need to start over again. But time may be running out. What to do? First pray, then go back through the scriptures and ask yourself, "What is the good news here?"

Now for some more percolating — are any themes emerging? Is there any sense of focus? Do you have a leading, a prompting from the Holy Spirit to go in this direction or that? It's like doing a jigsaw puzzle. You've got all the pieces; now is the time to begin to fit them together. The only difference is that unlike a puzzle, you are doing this usually without knowing what the picture on the box is. You are discerning it as you go. When you sense that you have a leading to go in a particular direction with a sermon, then you are ready for the next step.

Begin to order your material, that is, put it in sequence. I like to put things in a natural sequence, so that things flow. This is something you have to sense, to feel, just as when telling a story, you have to tell it in a certain sequence for it to make sense. So begin to put the items you jotted down in a sequence that makes sense to you. At this point you may discover that unlike the jigsaw puzzle, you have some pieces that belong to another puzzle, and you have to put them aside for another sermon another day. Don't try to make all your pieces fit. Usually about one-third to one-half

15

of what I have jotted down is never used. Here is probably one of the most helpful hints I can give to someone who is struggling to draft the first outline of a sermon: Keep to one sermon! You probably have enough material jotted down to write two, three, or even more sermons. Once you realize that you may be stuck because you are torn between two or more sermons, pick one, and get on with it.

Also, at this point do not focus on your beginning and your ending. If you have something you think will work for a beginning and/or ending, fine, but if not, don't worry about it. If you've got good solid content for the vast middle of the sermon, then order and sequence that content. We'll come back to the beginning and ending later.

I usually struggle with the sequencing of the main content. A common mistake here is to switch back and forth too much from one item to another. While going back and forth works when something is written and people can go back and visually look at it, verbal material, such as a sermon, must be kept very straightforward and simple, or the hearers will get lost. For example, I try not to switch back and forth too much between a biblical story and the points I am making. It may make more verbal sense to tell the whole Bible story, then make five points, rather than tell a bit of the Bible story, make a point, tell more of the Bible story, make another point, etc. Similarly, try not to break up major thoughts with minor ones. Do one thing at a time in your sermon. Keep it simple.

4. Just Tell The Story!

An effective way to preach, particularly on major feast days when the story speaks for itself, is simply to tell the gospel story. The most effective example I ever heard was an Easter day sermon that simply told the story of the women walking to the tomb, with some embellishment of what they might have been thinking or talking about; their discovery, with all the color and details described with imagination and care; and Jesus' approach in the garden. If all else fails, and you can't come up with a sermon, just retell the story with all the imagery you can.

5. Telling Jokes

I like to use jokes in sermons. They are especially effective at the beginning of a sermon to gain people's attention. Listeners are much more likely to stay with you if you start with a joke, versus saying, "This morning my sermon is taken from the ninth chapter of Judges." Here are some rules for good old-fashioned joke-telling in church:

a. It should not be offensive (sexist, racist, classist, etc.).

b. The point of the joke should directly connect to the point you are making. If it doesn't, perhaps you are using the joke just for a laugh. Don't.

c. It should not offend sensitive consciences (avoid jokes involving sex, drugs, alcohol, sacred religious subjects such as the Virgin Birth, etc.).

d. It should not be funny at anyone's expense (no fat jokes, dumb blonde jokes, etc.).

By this time you might think there aren't many jokes left to tell. Well, there's always that great stock of jokes that begins, "This guy died and went to heaven and saw Saint Peter there at the pearly gates...." So get it out of your system and tell lots of jokes when preaching on heaven.

6. Telling Real Stories

Telling real stories is good. Every sermon should have at least two stories that actually happened, and at least one of those should be really good. Here are a few tips for telling stories:

a. If you are telling a story that happened to you, then tell it in the first person. Be clear this is your story — besides they'll figure it out anyway if you don't. If there is something in the story that makes you look really bad, either take it out, clean it up a little, or, unless it's really, really bad, just tell it. People love to know that preachers are real people and they do stupid, dumb, and bad things. If it's a story that happens to make you look extra good, holy, and wonderful, then work in a little self-deprecating humor so they know you don't take yourself too seriously. I've even said, "I know you probably think I'm only telling this story because it makes me look good, but ..." and then smile. Many of us have the wrong-headed idea that we shouldn't preach using our own stories. While we do have to be careful that we don't get too self-oriented and bore people to death, most of us need to tell more good stories from our own experiences, not fewer.

b.   If you are telling a true story about somebody else, be clear about that too. If that someone else is in the church, absolutely get that person's permission first. If it's about someone else whom the parishioners might possibly know, change enough of the details so that the person's identity is forever protected, or, again, get that person's permission first. If it's about someone the parishioners could not possibly ever know, tell the story straight, except maybe change the person's name just as an extra fail-safe measure. Be very careful about telling stories of people identified as members of former churches of yours though, especially if the story does not reflect well on that person, because it raises the question in people's minds, "Will the preacher ever tell a story like this about me? Will my personal life stories show up in the preacher's sermons ten years from now in some church?"

c.   There are plenty of good "Once there was a little boy who ..." types of stories, stories that are cute, make people laugh, make a good point, are generic, and you don't have to worry about anyone thinking, "Hey, that's my story and the preacher didn't get my permission!" The only caution here is to be sensitive to your hearers. Over time, make sure you use some little girl stories, some young people stories,

18

some middle-aged people stories, some married folk stories, some old people stories, white people, black people, rich people, poor people stories too. Mix 'em up and don't get stuck in one mode.

d. Stories are great especially because most of us can tell a story without writing out a complete manuscript. You can just jot a few key ideas down, and then telling a story will allow you to give great eye contact. Generally telling a story also brings back those minds that have wandered off during your sermon.

e. Don't make up a story that sounds true but isn't, in order to fit the point you want to make. People will see through it. If you really can't find any story to illustrate your point, your point may not be so good or so true.

7. How Not To Begin

One bad thing that inexperienced clergy tend to do is to apologize for their sermons. I advise that you think about never doing this, for two reasons. First, if you sought the Holy Spirit's guidance on the sermon throughout the week, you ought to trust that. Second, the actual experience of many preachers is that most of the sermons they thought were pretty awful actually receive a goodly number of compliments — not that compliments are the measure of a sermon's worth. But preaching a sermon that you think is bad and getting compliments anyway does seem to be one way that God has devised to keep us preachers humble. If you didn't seek the Holy Spirit through the week, then deal with that between you and God, but trust that the sermon you came up with is the sermon the listeners need.

One exception might be if you were up all week with a sick spouse or child in the hospital. You are exhausted, and you basically have no sermon. Go ahead and apologize if that makes you feel better, but seriously, a short sermon, maybe even one relating how God ministered to you during that time, would be an incredibly effective sermon.

Another way not to begin is to take your listeners through all the ups and downs of writing your sermon. I simply remind you that you are not there to describe your process of sermon writing; you are there to preach the one sermon God gave you. When Michael Jordan shows up to play basketball, he shoots the ball; he doesn't stand around and describe to people how he practiced for hour upon hour. If you really labored on your sermon, talk about it with God. The people just aren't interested.

8. How Not To Close

If there is anything church people complain about, it is preachers who keep talking long after they should have stopped. So here are the basics to closing your sermon:

First, when you are done, stop talking.

Second, never lie about closing your sermon. There is the story of the little boy who went to a church where the pastor would say, "Now in closing ..." and proceed to preach for another half hour. One day the child asked his mom, "What does 'in closing' mean?" The mom answered: "Nothing."

Third, never introduce a new subject in your closing. Remember the old adage about public speaking: "Tell 'em what you're going to tell 'em, tell 'em, and then tell 'em what you told 'em." If you can't think of any other way to end your sermon, simply conclude by summarizing what you have been talking about for the last fifteen to twenty minutes.

Stay away from lettuce endings — you know, "Let us do this; let us do that." Occasionally lettuce is okay for dessert but a better way to end is with a fudge brownie, something that goes down more smoothly. Get your lettuce points in earlier on.

9. Bookends

The beginning and ending of your sermon are like bookends — they serve to hold up the content between them, and they are a matched set. Once you have your main content set, the last, and one of the most important things, to do is to put the beginning and the ending on the sermon. Work on them as a set. Just as a novel or a movie or a newspaper article signals the end is coming by referring to something (a phrase, an image, a musical interlude) from the beginning of the novel or movie or article, signal the upcoming end of your sermon by going back to something from the introduction. Sometimes early in the drafting process, you will have an idea for a story with which to begin or a quote with which to end, but put them aside until you are ready to work on them as matching bookends.

10. Practicing Out Loud

The best way to prepare is to tell the stories, either out loud or in your head, as many times as you like. Tell them to yourself until you've got all the pieces down — all the nuances, all the places to pause, all the body language. Practice the beginning and the ending. Get the sermon off the page and into your body.

11. A Title For Your Sermon

The very last thing to do is to give the sermon a title. I find that giving any attention to the title before I am completely finished is distracting. If by the end of writing the sermon the title is not crystal clear, probably the sermon is not very clear either.

Since I seldom get my title before 6 p.m. on Saturday, it is definitely not going to get into the bulletin for Sunday. I know it looks like you are organized, efficient, and on top of things to have your sermon title on the sign out front and in the bulletin for Sunday morning, but I would advise against it. Be open to the Spirit to the last minute, and this means — you don't have a title for anybody but yourself most of the time.

12. Finally, Number The Pages

If you have more than one page, number your pages so they can be easily read. More than once, due to an ill wind or an enthusiastic acolyte, my pages have gotten out of order, and I have been saved by having numbered the pages.

Also, upon occasion, a well-meaning layperson, straightening up the church, or picking up bulletins, will pick up your sermon and move it. Meanwhile some of the pages get shuffled. You go to preach at the second service, and you look down and your conclusion is on top. When the pages are numbered, you can easily rearrange them.

I have also heard that some clergy like to play tricks on other clergy and shuffle the sermon pages when the preacher is not looking.

13. Last Minute Changes

About twice a year, I go to bed on Saturday night with my sermon finished and ready to go on Sunday. And then God messes with my head. Sometimes God actually gives me, point by point, another sermon. Sometimes I have a dream and when I wake up, I know that I have to change the sermon in a major way. I do not fret about this. I trust it and I do it.

Other times, I go to bed with the sermon finished, but then I am restless about it, tossing and turning, fussing about the sermon. I pray that God would let me go to sleep. I can change the sermon in the morning if I have to.

Sometimes I preach the sermon at the early service and realize that it needs some work. Often this is minor — it is usually a matter of sequence — I see that this point needs to go before that one, or this story goes before that story. Other times, I have done major reconstructive surgery on the sermon between services. But I only do this if I feel absolutely sure of the changes I am making. Otherwise, it's best to trust the process, preach it as it is, and make changes afterwards.

It is usually not until I have preached a sermon that I see "what needs fixing." I will write these changes into the sermon in the margins after the service so that when I look at the sermon in the future, I have already written down what I think I need to do to make it more effective.

three

A Great Delivery

1. The Purpose Of A Sermon

The purpose of a sermon is to transmit emotion. I would borrow the words of A. E. Housman, a poet, who wrote about the purpose of poetry: "To transmit emotion — not to transmit thought but to set up in the reader's sense a vibration corresponding to what was felt by the writer — is the particular function of poetry."[1]

A sermon does, or should do, the same thing — it should transmit the emotion of the preacher, or more accurately, the emotion/energy of the Holy Spirit as expressed through the preacher. Yes, there are definitely thoughts, ideas, facts, and theology to get across. But they won't stick with the people past the final prayer (or, let's be honest, the "Amen" after the sermon) unless they have been transmitted on an emotional plane.

Another way to describe the purpose of a sermon is this: a sermon teaches people how to pray. I do not mean in a narrow, explicit sense, but in a broad sense. A sermon should teach the hearer something about his or her relationship with God — and if it does that, then it should be conveying something about the intimacy that is part of that relationship. Sometimes when I am stuck writing a sermon, I ask myself how in the world might this help someone to pray better? And the answer often gives me the focus I need to refocus and finish writing the sermon.

2. Before Starting

Approach the pulpit (or the spot from which you will preach) slowly, deliberately, and with a good mix of confidence and humility. Your notes should be set; don't shuffle them. Before you start,

23

pray silently for God's strength to come into you to preach the sermon with power (or a dose of whatever else you think you need that day). Then you can do wonders for the receptivity of your sermon by simply smiling. Look out over the folks who will put up with your sermon today, whether five or five hundred, and stand amazed that you are God's messenger. Smile that you have such an awesome vocation. Soak it in. What a privilege it is to preach!

3. Invocations — Prayers Before The Sermon

It is common in some churches to say a "set" prayer before the start of the sermon. Below are some of my favorites. While they can be read, I much prefer to memorize them and pray them with great conviction and power. They probably do as much for me in setting the tone as they do for the people.

"May the words of my mouth and the meditations of our hearts be always acceptable in your sight, O God, our strength and our redeemer."

+++

"What we hear with our ears and say with our lips, may we take to our hearts and show forth in our lives, for Christ's sake, Amen." (Warning — make sure you do *not* say, "What we hear with our lips" or some other mix-up — you have to be alert and think when saying this one.)

+++

A good invocation for Advent:
"Lord Jesus Christ, at your first coming John the Baptist prepared the way for you. Grant that my preaching may also prepare and make ready the way for you to come and turn our hearts, so that at your second coming to judge the world, we may be found acceptable in your sight."

+++

24

An invocation for Pentecost, and for sermons emphasizing the person and work of the Holy Spirit:

"Come, Holy Spirit, fill the hearts of your faithful, and kindle in us the fire of your love."

+++

Good for feast days:

"May God send forth the Word, and may the spices of the gospel melt to give forth their sweet fragrance. [May the word of God become more to us than gold or precious stone, and sweeter than honey in the honeycomb.]"

+++

A basic standby:

"May the Word of God be spoken.
May the Word of God be heard.
May the Word of God be understood,
through Jesus Christ who is the Word."

+++

Also good for Pentecost:

"May our eyes catch fire and see God,
May our ears catch fire and hear God,
May our minds catch fire and know God,
May our tongues catch fire and name God,
May our hearts catch fire and love God."

+++

A good invocation for Epiphany:

"May Jesus Christ, the king of glory, help us to make the right use of all the myrrh that God sends, and to offer to him the true incense of our hearts, for his name's sake. Amen."

+++

This is adapted from Ephesians 6:19-20:
"Pray for me,
that I may be granted the right words when I open my mouth,
and may boldly and freely make known
God's hidden purpose,
for which I am an ambassador.
Pray that I may speak of it boldly,
as it is my duty to speak. Amen."

4. Great Beginnings

Memorize your opening line(s). This will get you off to a great start with direct eye contact. Whether it's a story, a joke, a quote, a verse of scripture, a question, it should lead directly into the subject matter of the sermon. You do not have to be cute here. But start with confidence in your opener. And keep smiling.

5. Preaching With Notes

In my earlier preaching days, I would rough out the sermon, then go back and write out a very readable outline. As I finished up more and more sermons late on Saturday or early Sunday, I began to forego writing out my notes in a nice outline. I began taking my yellow legal pad with me with all my notes scribbled here and there, with whole sections crossed out and margin notes and abbreviations and arrows all over. It works for me but I don't recommend it. I prefer to make a clean, readable outline of my notes, especially now that I need reading glasses. If the light is not just right, scribbled notes cannot be read.

The outline is simple: the main thought that is the opener, then the first main section, with maybe a couple of sub-points. I don't write out whole stories. If I am going to tell the story about getting lost out in the country and having to turn the car around and how that is an example of what repentance is, I might just jot down on my legal pad "story of getting lost out in country — define repentance."

The outline generally fits on one page; sometimes it takes two. If I am using more paper than that, it is probably more of a manuscript than an outline. Except for certain occasions, I think manuscript sermons probably aren't what people today need or want.

People are used to ten-second sound bites on radio and television, not listening to dissertations of twenty or fifteen or even twelve minutes' duration.

Preachers today must engage the listener, and that means getting unshackled from a manuscript. You can begin with small steps, telling stories that have happened to you without reading word by word from a manuscript. Then expand until more and more of your sermon is delivered from an outline, not the full manuscript.

6. Preaching Without Notes

To do this, you have to have a very simple one-two-three sermon. It needs to flow so that even if you get distracted, you could pick up the story because it flows in a natural sequence.

The thing most preachers who preach without notes worry about is that they will suddenly lose their place and have absolutely nothing to look down at to refresh their memory. That has happened to me a few times and most of the time, after the initial panic, the train of thought comes back, just as it does in everyday life. The worst that happens is you have to ask the congregation, "Now, where was I?" They are happy to oblige.

I don't think it is any great emblem on your shoulder if you can preach without notes. Personally, I am more comfortable having the outline in front of me. Even though I may only glance at it a few times, it is a security blanket that allows me to funnel all my energy into preaching the sermon, rather than getting stressed out over trying to remember where the sermon is going. But if you enjoy the challenge of preaching without notes, go for it.

The other main thing I had to get over without notes was, what if I make a mistake? What if I say something heretical? I made a decision a few years ago that I would rather preach without a manuscript and perhaps say some really stupid things, than to preach with a nice safe manuscript that I had checked for theological or historical or other errors. So far, the worst I've said was that Joseph was the youngest son of Jacob (he wasn't — Benjamin was) and that Paul and Barnabas were in prison together (it was Paul and Silas). I would rather make these kinds of mistakes and give an engaged, energetic sermon, than a safe sermon from a perfect manuscript.

7. The Remote Control Test

I have noticed something about a number of the preachers on television on Sunday mornings and afternoons. A lot of them are saying loving, wonderful things about God. But something doesn't feel right inside me. If I don't feel too good in my stomach, that is probably a clue that something is wrong. So I have developed a little test. So far it has been 100 percent accurate. I dig out the remote control from between the couch cushions, aim it at Super Preacher, and press the mute button. Then, without the sound, I can be totally attentive to the look on Super Preacher's face. This way, what is coming out of his or her mouth doesn't confuse me. If the preacher looks loving, kind, and nice, I press the mute button again to turn the sound back on, and I listen. On the other hand, if the preacher looks mean, or if he or she looks angry, or seems to be shouting at me, then I go to another channel. I do not think that a preacher should look mean or mad, or yell at his listeners.

When I am preaching sometimes I think, what are people seeing on my face? Could I pass the remote control test? I want them to see my loving face, even if I am preaching about repentance or death. Besides, that is the only way they will hear me. If I do not love them with my face, then in their hearts and heads they are going to turn on their internal "mute" button, and nothing I say will get through anyway. So smile and love them.

8. Words That Should Not Be Used Under Any Circumstances

This is the story of just about the biggest goober I ever made preaching. I wanted to tell a story about how I was really frustrated and upset and angry. I thought I would use a new phrase that I had heard a few times recently. I wasn't entirely sure that it meant frustrated, angry, and upset, but since it was quite clearly used in that context several times by others, I just thought I'd go ahead and use it. So in my sermon I just happened to mention, with an entirely straight face, that recently I had been "on the rag." I assumed it was the cousin to "on a tear" or "on a rampage," and besides that, it sounded pretty cool, I thought, so I threw it out there in my sermon.

Afterward, a young woman about my age shook my hand and greeted me and whispered in my ear, "Do you know the meaning of what you said this morning?" I looked at her puzzled, and asked, "Uh, what?" She told me in no uncertain terms. I do not think I have been closer to total mortification in any other circumstance in life.

Which brings me to the general subject of "Words and phrases that should not be used in a sermon under any circumstances." Note that "any" means "any." Those words would include: intercourse, erection, pubic, ejaculate or ejaculatory, and copulation. In fact, it's probably a good idea to expunge any "bathroom talk" or language about private bodily functions from sermons as a general rule.

That said, the fastest, most sure-proof way to bring back a congregation that is falling asleep under your preaching is to say "sex" in the middle of your sermon. At once, as if manipulated by a string, all the heads that were nodding down to doze, peek at the bulletin, look for a nail file in a purse, and examine the number of squares in the carpet (yes, it is possible for a sermon to be so boring that counting the number of squares in the carpet a dozen times is more interesting than anything that is being said), yes, all those heads snap up and all eyes are fixated for one luscious moment on the pulpit (use this secret weapon wisely).

9. Speeding Up A Notch

I always have mixed feelings when I am a passenger on a commercial airline that for one reason or another has gotten out of the gate late and I am sitting there eating one of the 22 peanuts in the bag when the pilot's voice comes over the audio system crackling with interference and says, "Well, everybody, welcome to the flight today. We got out of the gate a little later than planned there because of some (tzzzztskkkkkk) repairs to the (tzzzzzskkkkk) but now that we are airborn, copilot Joe and I here are going to kick up the speed a notch and try to make up some of that time, so, if everything goes well, we should be arriving on time at our destination. Sit back and enjoy the flight."

Would somebody please explain to me why, if it is possible to go faster under these circumstances, they don't fly at this increased speed all the time? What are they doing up there ... holding back on normal flights just so they have a little room to "kick it up a notch" when they are running late?

Now, let me say that sometimes I am tempted to do the same thing in my preaching. The service got started late, the hymns were extra long, the people are looking not happy that they might get to their tee time a few minutes late, so I am tempted to get up in the pulpit and "kick it up a notch." I think it's important to resist that temptation. Sure, probably all my sermons could be reduced by 75 percent and we could get to the end of the service faster. But that's not the point. So sit back and break out the peanuts, folks, you are getting the whole nine yards today.

10. Harkey

On the other hand, I have always been mindful that a good sermon ends on time. I suppose I learned this at an early age when I sat with my mother in the last pew to the pastor's left, which happened to be the closest seat to the exit door, a fact I did not fully appreciate until one day when I was doing a little self-psychoanalyzing, trying to figure out why I did not like people who sat in the last pew and left the service just as fast as they could, but I digress ...

As my feet swung in front of me because I was too short to put my feet on the nice carpet below, my view from the pew included Harkey, the head usher who had been a church fixture as long as I could remember. Harkey was old and tall and skinny and bent over and he sat in a folding chair with the rest of the ushers behind the last pew, square in the center aisle. I realized in later years that this was an ideal spot from which to flag the preacher if he (and it was a "he" in those days) went overtime. "Overtime" was 12:01. If Pastor Brown hadn't wound it up by then (the sermon was the last item before the final prayer), Harkey's big pocket watch which he kept in his vest would go off, and my mother would turn to me, nod in the pastor's direction, and say, "I hope he hurries up, or my roast chicken is going to burn." And I too silently rooted for the sermon to end quickly, so we could be first out the door to greet the pastor, run down the cement steps, and ride home to roast chicken, dressing, and mashed potatoes. So even now, when I start to get a little long-winded, I swear I start to smell roast chicken burning and I can hear Harkey shuffling to turn off his pocket watch, and I wrap things up real fast.

11. Great Endings

The ending of your sermon should be memorized so that you can give it while looking up and out. It should be delivered with a "punch" unless that's clearly inappropriate. Again, you should work hard at having a smile on your face at this point.

Before your final "amen," pause. Say "amen" like you mean it. Don't shuffle with your notes and don't hurry out of the pulpit. Naturally and deliberately return to your place.

Then try to forget about it. I'll be honest. If I think I preached a really good sermon or a really bad one, I am usually still thinking about it right through the rest of the service. If it didn't flow as well as I thought, I am trying to figure out how to fix it. But by doing this, I miss the rest of the service. Try as hard as you can to put it out of your head. You have all the rest of Sunday to think about it if you want to. Let it go and enjoy your own service.

12. Three Sermons

There is an old saying that every time you preach, there are three sermons:

a. The sermon you intended to deliver;
b. The sermon you actually delivered;
c. The sermon you wish you had delivered.

Get over it.

---

1. A. E. Housman, "The Name and Nature of Poetry," *The Messages of the Poets* (New York: Charles Scribner's Sons, 1911), p. 236.

four

Stuff They Never Teach You

1. First Sermon

The first sermon I ever preached was as a layperson in a small rural church in New York State. I think I preached on one of the Psalms. I don't remember anything else about it, except that it was an old church and it did not even have a toilet. I'll be honest with you — not having toilet facilities impacts a person's sermons in more ways than one.

Your first sermon is going to ramble all over the place, toilet or not. But eventually, you'll start to get better.

2. The Most Important Advice About Preaching That You Will Ever Receive

I am about to share with you the most important advice about preaching that you will ever receive. It alone will justify the purchasing of this book. At first it may not appear to you to be the most important advice, but I assure you that it is. Some day, you will thank me. My advice is this: Before you leave the vesting room to go preach, look in the mirror, smile, and make sure that you don't have pieces of food in your teeth. You will look pretty ridiculous if you have poppy seeds from your morning bagel sticking to your front tooth, or a big piece of green lettuce dangling from your incisor. Or, frankly, something worse: I am visualizing a male preacher with a beard who has a cold — enough said.

3. Pulling Pork From The Barrel

Once I asked a colleague what he would be preaching on the next Sunday. "Oh," said he, "I think I'm going to pull some pork out of the barrel." Recognizing this as a vague political term, I asked him exactly what that meant. He replied, "That means I'm preaching an old sermon I've already got in the file."

I have to say I have mixed feelings about preaching old sermons. I remember my disgust as a young pastor when one day the preacher for the day arrived in the sacristy to vest, and put his sermon notes down on the table. They were, no kidding, yellow. I thought to myself, "Can't you even copy the sermon on fresh paper? This is awful." However, I have to be honest and say, it was a very good sermon. A classic. Worthy of being repeated. So why should the preacher have bothered to write another sermon when the one he had was perfectly appropriate?

You can also imagine my surprise when some parishioners informed me that one of my predecessors had exactly 52 sermons. Yup, 52 sermons, one for each Sunday of the year, and he repeated them over and over during his tenure. They knew his sermons pretty well, and, I understand, used the sermon time after a while to catch up on sleep.

My conviction is this: We preachers need to be getting fresh sermons from the Holy Spirit each week — that's our vocation and our privilege, our ministry and our job. We should be working hard to discern God's word for today for the people to whom we are preaching. That said, however, there are some times to pull the pork out of the barrel. One, as I've mentioned, is when you have a terrific sermon. Like a good recipe, why bother to try to improve on it? Just keep serving it up as often as you can. Serve it to different groups, if you can, but serve it up. Second, there are those weeks when either you are out of town all week, or completely absorbed in gut-wrenching pastoral work, or have some major sickness or family problem that draws all your energy and leaves you feeling pretty dry, without much energy to write a sermon. If those circumstances happen, then pulling some pork out of the barrel makes sense. (Make sure you update any examples or stories you have so it's not totally obvious to everyone that you are reusing an old sermon). However, if this is happening more than three or four times a year, you are pulling too much pork.

4. Bad Hair Day Sermons

Occasionally you want to crawl out of the pulpit on your hands and knees and head for the nearest hole. Sometimes sermons turn out bad. They fall flat. It doesn't make any sense to you, and you wrote the thing! You need to know this happens.

Think about a bad sermon in terms of baking a recipe. Most of the time it comes out swell. But sometimes you undercook it or overcook (a.k.a. burn) it. If you forget one key ingredient, like yeast or baking powder, the whole thing will fall flat. Or you forget to grease the bottom of the pans and everything sticks. See all this as a learning process. It happens to the best preachers, just like striking out happens to the best hitters. Go back to the dugout and get ready for the next time at the plate.

5. Hazards Of The Remote Microphone

Here is maybe the second little piece of advice that frankly may save you your job some day. So many churches these days use lapel microphones, and what a blessing they are as they force all those who sit in the back pew to actually have to hear your sermon rather than escape it. (Before the invention of lapel mikes, it was a known fact that older women who were hard of hearing would sit in the back three pews and then proceed to complain — very loudly — that they could not hear the sermon.)

You will want to find the "off" position on your friendly mike and commit it to memory. I have heard terrible tales of preachers who, following the sermon, ducked into the bathroom to take care of some emergency personal business, such as vomiting or urinating. However, they forgot to turn off their lapel mike, and these unpleasant and rather personal sounds were then broadcast throughout the church.

6. When You Get The Giggles

As any youngster knows, the worst place to get the giggles is in church, because once you get them, there is no stopping them. Things in church are hilariously funny once you start on a giggly roll.

Sometimes it happens during the reading of the lessons. A typo, a mispronunciation, and there is a titter throughout the congregation. One time, the scripture reading was from Timothy, and the reader said, "Now unto God immoral, the only-wise God...." The all-time winner for bad pronunciation has to be the poor lay reader who was stuck with an Old Testament reading that included the Hittites, the Philistines, and the Jebusites. The challenged reader made it through the list only to pronounce the last group as the "Jebu-zitties."

Sometimes it's the bulletin announcements. Since entire books have been published on unintentionally humorous bulletin announcements, I won't go into details here. My advice is simply not to read the bulletin announcements until after the sermon!

Sometimes it's pure human drama. In one moment of total silence between readings, a person passed air in a very loud way. Everyone in the entire church heard it, and the place was on the brink of an uproar, so as I stood up to read the Gospel, I simply said, "Okay, let's all laugh and just get it out real good." When they finally stopped laughing, they and I could go on.

Sometimes only the preacher gets the giggles. This has happened to me only one time. I was seated in a pew next to a tall, lanky fellow named John, and I simply buried my head in his stomach and laughed until I stopped. What anybody else thought, I don't know, but it was the beginning of a good friendship with the gentleman who lent me his tummy.

7. What To Do If You Forget To Bring Your Sermon

This pretty much happens to everybody sooner or later. You will be in your car on the way to church, or worse, processing into church at the start of the service, and you will realize that you and your sermon notes are not in the same place. The first time this happens, it could cause an anxiety attack. However, there is no need to panic. Simply do this: write down your three main points. If your sermon has any organization and flow to it, you should be able to remember at least one major illustration or story for each main point. Jot down these main points, and the key words to remind you of the illustrations, on a piece of paper. These are now your sermon notes. Wing it the best you can. Don't apologize for losing your notes or even tell them you did. And here it a little secret: I am willing to bet you will get more positive feedback than you usually do. That's just the way it works.

I recommend "pretending" you have lost your sermon notes each week in preparation for the big day. It can be a little game to play with yourself, especially if you have a long commute to church. On the serious side, it is also one of the single most helpful exercises I can think of doing when your sermon is written but you really aren't happy with it, because that may be a clue it really doesn't flow well. If you pretend that you have forgotten your notes, it will help you to reduce your convoluted and wordy sermon down to three or so main points which do have some clarity and connection.

8. Pages Out Of Order?

Even if you number your pages, things can go wrong. I have heard about an ordination service where the preacher's notes were subterfuged by his colleagues — when he got to the pulpit, the pages were all out of order. Or, every so often, a page turns up missing — you are in the middle of the sermon when you realize you are missing a whole page. There's not a whole lot to do at this point except grin and bear it, try to fix it, and if you can't, wing it as best you can.

9. What Time Is It? — And Other Questions To Ask

Stirred up and chest puffed out one fine first Sunday of Advent, I began my sermon about the end times and knowing the times and seasons by bellowing out a stirring, rhetorical question appropriate for Advent: "Do you know what time it is?" In the stupendous silence that followed, a small male voice in the front pew said, "It's ten after eight."

Beware: If you ask a question, somebody just might answer it.

Since I often preach from the center aisle, and sometimes ask questions, I do get answers. If they are biblical knowledge sorts of questions, I usually have a long wait before some tentative guesses are offered. If they are more everyday kinds of questions, people generally speak up with their best guesses to my questions.

Occasionally, someone raises a hand or asks me a question straight out. In that case, I just answer it the best I can and if it looks like trouble, I don't give any more eye contact in that direction!

five

Preaching The Big Days
Of The Church Year

1. Smile And Don't Yell

A few years ago there was a well-known clergyperson, an author and theologian, on one of the television morning shows at Christmastime. One of the weekday morning show hosts asked the priest to give some advice for clergy preaching at that busy time of year, when all kinds of new and old faces suddenly show up at church services. The clergyperson smiled and said that clergy should smile a lot, be nice, and not yell at people who haven't been to church since last Christmas, etc.

That is not bad advice as far as it goes. But I would like to go a bit further and actually offer some substance on how to preach the big days. The best advice I have is: be short and to the point in your sermon. In this chapter you will find some of my favorite and most loved material to use on the great days of the church year.

2. Preaching The Incarnation

Stay away from thick theological language and focus on "Immanuel," which means "God with us." As with all sermons on the big days of the church year, a short and to-the-point sermon usually works well. Here are some sample stories appropriate for Christmas Eve/Day:

a. Will God really dwell on earth with us?

At the celebration and dedication of Solomon's temple, Solomon prays and asks God a question: Will God really dwell on earth with people? Christmas gives the definitive answer: yes!

39

Christmas is our opportunity to proclaim that the Word became flesh and dwelt among us; literally, he pitched his tent and dwelt among us. Or as the *Message Bible* says, "The Word became flesh and moved into the neighborhood" (John 1:14).

At the entrance to the Church of the Nativity in Bethlehem in the Holy Land, there is a large sign that lists numerous rules for tourists and visitors to follow. Rules like: "No weapons allowed," "No smoking," and "No loitering." One of the rules caught my attention. It said, "Must wear decent attire," except "decent" was, like many words on signs in English in the Holy Land, spelled incorrectly. It was spelled "d-e-s-c-e-n-t." Must wear descent attire! How appropriate! That is what Jesus wore on Christmas — he wore his descent attire — he came to dwell on earth with men and women.

b. Somebody with skin on 'em[1]

The parents of a little girl threw a dinner party for friends. While the adults were downstairs enjoying themselves, the little girl was upstairs in her bedroom. After a while, she came to the balcony and said, "Mommy! I'm lonely up here." Mom answered her, "Don't worry honey, Daddy and I will be up in a while." After another half hour had passed, she reappeared and said from the balcony, "Mommy! I'm all alone up here!" Mom comforted her with words of assurance that she would be okay. A third time she appeared at the balcony and said, "Mommy! I'm all alone up here and I'm afraid." Mom said, "Honey, you're not alone, God is with you." The little girl replied, "Yes, I know, but I want somebody with some skin on 'em!"

Christmas is when Jesus put on our skin and came to live among us.

c. The Day God Grunted[2]

A couple in the southwestern part of the United States had a young daughter who was quite a troublesome child. She was in trouble at school, she was in trouble with the police, she was in trouble with her friends, and most of all, she was in trouble with her parents. Things had gotten so bad that the daughter would not even talk to her folks — not one word.

The couple took their daughter to a well-known psychiatrist in the Midwest to get help, but to no avail. Then they found a psychiatrist who was willing to try to help, but he would see her only three times and no more. The parents agreed to give it a try.

At the first session, the girl would not say one word; so the psychiatrist and the little girl sat in silence for the whole hour. The second session started the same way, but after thirty minutes the girl made a little grunt. The doctor grunted back. And the session ended. At the third and final session, twenty minutes went by, and the girl grunted. The doctor grunted. She grunted; the doctor grunted again. Then the girl looked into the doctor's eyes and asked, "Why are you making grunting sounds?" This was the breakthrough the doctor was hoping for. And the two went on to talk to each other and the psychiatrist was eventually able to help the troubled young girl.

I believe this is a Christmas story, a story of the incarnation. You see, the girl and the doctor were worlds apart. She wasn't even speaking; he was a learned man with a Ph.D. in psychiatry. How could they communicate and have a relationship? Humans have the same problem. How could limited, finite, vulnerable humans ever hope to communicate with an unlimited, all-knowing, all-powerful God?

But the doctor bridged that communication gap by responding to the girl on her terms, in a way that she felt comfortable with, in a way that she could receive. God did the same thing at Christmas. God bridged the gap between divinity and humanity by communicating with us in our own language, on our own terms: God took on flesh and became human, coming to us as a baby. God sent Jesus to share our human nature, to live and die as one of us.

Finally, the doctor was not afraid to risk looking stupid. At first, even the girl thought he was a little ridiculous. "Why are you making those grunting sounds?" she asked. And to anyone who might be looking on, it all looked like a pretty ridiculous thing for the doctor to be grunting at this girl. But the doctor was willing to do whatever it took to get through to her.

When God sent Jesus into the world as a baby, God risked looking stupid too. People still say things sometimes like, "How can a baby be the God of the universe? That's ridiculous. Christianity is ridiculous." But God was willing to do whatever it took to get through to us humans.

So that's why I like to tell people that Christmas is the day God grunted. By sending the baby Jesus, God did break through to us, and the world has not been the same since.

d. Chugga[3]

Translating from one language to another is difficult work. First there is the problem of idioms. If I say, "She was up in the air about selling the house," the translator cannot literally translate the phrase "up in the air," but has to find another phrase so that the hearer can understand that the woman was undecided about selling the house. Secondly, there is the problem of words for emotions. Certain Chinese dialects, for example, have no words for angry, sad, or joyful — so how do you translate those words into a language that has no words to express them? A third difficulty is translating across cultures. For example, how do you translate the word "king" for an African tribunal that rules itself by a council and has no concept of what a king is?

One day, a Bible translator in Africa who had worked on many translations picked up a recently translated version of the Bible. It was in Chugga, a little known dialect in his home country in the Democratic Republic of Congo (formerly Zaire). As he read it, he began to cry. Chugga was the language he had used growing up. His mother had taught him to pray in Chugga. Still when he prayed, although he was a learned man who knew many different languages, he thought and prayed in his native tongue of Chugga. To read the Bible in Chugga, his native tongue, was such a joy that he couldn't hold back the tears.

There is nothing quite like hearing or reading something in your own language. If you've ever traveled to a non-English speaking country, you know as a tourist how your ears perk up when someone is speaking English.

God, too, is a translator of sorts. He faced a difficult translation problem — perhaps the most difficult of all. How could Divinity communicate with humanity? How could the Unlimited communicate with the limited, the Infinite one with finite human beings? How could a powerful God connect with vulnerable humanity? How could God make God's love and goodness known to us?

First God spoke to us through creation. Then God formed a relationship with the people of Israel. Through a covenant and the Ten Commandments, Israel became God's holy people. Then God communicated by the word spoken through the prophets, as they proclaimed God's love, mercy, justice, compassion, and forgiveness. But still God could not fully bridge the communication gap.

Christmas is when God broke the communication barrier and solved the translation problem by communicating with us in the language we know best, the language we sleep and think and dream and walk and live in — the language of being human. God sent Jesus into the world as a human being. Jesus is the perfect translation of divinity into humanity.

When we celebrate Christmas, we are celebrating that God's work as a translator was successful, and like the man who cried for joy to read in his native language of Chugga, we rejoice that God chose to communicate with us in the language we are intimately familiar with — the language of being human.

3. Preaching Ash Wednesday

If I had my druthers, this is how I would preach on Ash Wednesday:

First I would tell the story of the little boy who went to church with his parents and listened to the sermon. When they got home, he went to his room for a while, and then came to his mother. "Mom," he asked, "is it true what the preacher said, that we came from dust and to dust we shall return?" The mom was amazed that her son had gotten the message so clearly. "Why, son, you are so good, you really listened tonight. Yes, it is true that we came from dust and to dust we return." "Well," the little boy said, "you'd better come up and look under my bed. There's a whole lot of people coming and going!"

43

Now for the serious part. First of all, it's no longer in vogue to preach on giving something up for Lent. The newfangled idea is to preach on "taking something on" instead. That is a bunch of bunk. Here Lent is about the only time we can preach on self-sacrifice, and we are throwing that down the tubes too. We need to get back to preaching on giving something up for Lent, and explaining it rightly.

To wit: every year I give up something. It may involve some food item, like dessert (if not several desserts a day) or chocolate or meat. It almost always involves giving up coffee. Some years I have given up varying amounts of watching television, swearing, and money to charities. Probably the best year was the year I gave up guessing people's motives. It saved me a lot of time.

Secondly, once you give up something, temptation comes at you from all angles. The year I gave up chocolate, I was attacked by chocolate. Ash Wednesday was barely ten hours old when I remembered that I had stashed some candy bars and some Oreos in the back of the cupboard. And immediately the thought came to mind: I had better eat them *right* now. If I wait forty days until Lent is over, they will be stale. Yes, I know I gave up chocolate, but I don't want to *waste* food (I was able to overcome this temptation when I realized that whether I threw that chocolate and those Oreo cookies out, or whether I ate them, they were going to waste either way).

I believe Satan enlists other people to help him tempt you. On the second Sunday of Lent in the year I gave up chocolate, one of my parishioners showed up at the door with a homemade German chocolate cake, my very favorite. I even encountered chocolate in the most unexpected places: I was getting my teeth cleaned and my dentist asked, "Do you want to try the new chocolate polish?"

Everything in my body rebels against giving something up. By 9 a.m. on the day after Ash Wednesday, the voice inside my head starts to plead, "I need that chocolate." Then, later, "I deserve that chocolate." And finally, "I cannot live without chocolate!"

Now we are at a good place, because Lent is not about some personal "home improvement project" to make me a better person, i.e., one who can actually resist chocolate. Nor is it about making me a slimmer person. Oh, that we would all get to Good Friday with slimmer waistlines. Oh, that we would all get to the end of Lent in better health, with better diets, with better use of our grocery money. But that is not what giving up something is about.

The purpose of giving something up is not to deaden our senses, to pretend that we aren't hungry when we are; it's not to pretend that we don't want to take a whole tub of ice cream and shovel our way through the whole thing *right* now. The purpose is not to deny ourselves and deaden our senses.

Here is the secret of Lent: the purpose of giving something up is to sharpen our senses. It is to realize, "I am really hungry." Or in my case, "I am dying for a cup of coffee. I'd give anything for a Snickers bar right now." And then to sit with it. To sit with the thirst, the hunger, the emptiness, the loneliness, and let it be real. To feel the pain, befriend it, and embrace it. And then the most important step: to invite God into that vacuum. "Oh, God, I'd love a cup of coffee this morning, but how much more so, oh God, do I need *you*! Come and fill me, fill me up, I am empty, Lord, and I need *you*!" The key is to become empty so that God can fill us up.

And then I suggest even one more step, one which will sanctify and make your sacrifice all the more holy: offer up that pain (Okay, I know this sounds overstated. After all, we are not in the third world and my not having a cup of coffee or some chocolate is hardly worthy of the word "pain" — but don't knock it until you've lived through that pain) — offer up that pain of yours on behalf of someone else and pray to God that that person's pain, whether it be physical, emotional, or other, may be lessened. God can make an exchange like that in the heavenlies if you only ask.

And that is how I would preach Ash Wednesday.

4. Preaching Palm Sunday

Palm Sunday is still one of the best attended Sundays, so you want to reach the folks who come every week as well as the ones who haven't been to church for a while but are sticking their toes in to see if the water is warm. The task of a Palm Sunday sermon is very simple: to get Jesus up on the cross. You need to move people from the Hosannas and waving of palm branches and singing, "All glory, laud, and honor," to people visualizing, even experiencing, Jesus hanging on the cross. The best story I have for doing that on Palm Sunday is a story about some young boys in Paris. I am told it is a true story, but it's a hand-me-down story whose origins I don't know.

One day, three young fellows wandered into the Cathedral of Notre Dame in Paris. They weren't Christians going to worship, but rather they were troublemakers, looking for a way to make fun of the worshipers.

One made a bet that he could imitate the parishioners and that no one would ever know that he wasn't even a Christian.

The other two fellows took him up on it. So the first fellow watched what everyone else was doing and followed suit. He crossed himself. He genuflected. He mouthed the prayers. When time came for communion, he went up to the altar to communion and opened his mouth for the wafer and received just like everyone else. So far, so good.

In those days, everyone went to confession after church, and so to follow through on his bet, he followed along. He overheard a fellow confess his sins, then he made up a list of sins of his own to confess, went into the confessional, and told it to the priest. For penance, the priest told him to come back alone that night, to stand before the large crucifix of Jesus, and to say three times, "You did all of this for me, and I don't give a damn."

Determined to keep and win the bet, the fellow did go back later that night. He walked up the long aisle in the dark until he stood in front of the crucifix.

Looking up at Jesus hanging there on the cross, he said,

"Jesus, you did all this for me, and I don't give a damn."

"Jesus, you did all this for me, and I don't give a damn."

"Jesus, you did all this for me ..."

In that moment, the reality of Jesus' death on the cross hit this fellow with all its force. He would never be the same again. On that day he became a disciple of the Crucified One. And that same young man later became the Archbishop of Paris.

That's what Palm Sunday is about: pausing long enough to stand before the cross and look at it, really *look* at it.

Postscript: Since most of the parishioners will probably not come to the Good Friday service, but pass go, collect $200, and go directly to Easter day, I think we may also want to accomplish the purpose of Good Friday's sermon (see below).

5. Preaching Good Friday

Whether you preach at a "Stations of the Cross" service, or a three-hour "Last seven words from the Cross," or have a short ten-minute homily on Good Friday, you have only one task: get Jesus in the grave.

Once you have done that, here is a favorite story of mine, called "The Room."[4]

In that place between wakefulness and dreams, I found myself in "The Room." There were no distinguishing features save for the one wall covered with small index card files. They were like the ones in libraries that list titles by author or subject in alphabetical order. But these files, which stretched from floor to ceiling and seemingly endlessly in every direction, had very different headings. As I drew near the wall of files, the first to catch my attention was the one that read "People I Have Liked." I opened it and began flipping through the cards. I quickly shut it, shocked to realize that I recognized the names written on each one. And then, without being told, I knew exactly where I was. This lifeless room with its small files was a crude catalog system for my life. Here were written the actions of my every moment, big and small, in a detail my memory couldn't match.

A sense of wonder and curiosity, coupled with horror, stirred within me as I began randomly opening files and exploring their content. Some brought joy and sweet memories, others a sense of shame and regret so intense that I would look over my shoulder to see if anyone was watching.

A file named "Friends" was next to the one marked "Friends I Have Betrayed." The titles ranged from the mundane to the outright weird: "Books I Have Read," "Lies I Have Told," "Comforts I Have Given," "Jokes I Have Laughed At." Some were almost hilarious in their exactness: "Things I Have Yelled At My Coworkers." Others I couldn't laugh at: "Things I Have Done In My Anger," "Things I Have Muttered Under My Breath About My Children." I never ceased to be surprised by the content. Often there were many more cards than I expected. Sometimes fewer than I hoped. I was overwhelmed by the sheer volume of the life I had lived.

Could it be possible that I had the time to write each of these thousands or even millions of cards? But each card confirmed this truth. Each card was written in my own handwriting and signed with my own signature.

When I pulled out the file marked "Movies I Have Watched," I realized the files grew to contain their contents. The cards were packed tightly, and yet after two or three yards of cards, I still hadn't found the end of the file. I shut it, shamed not so much by the content of the shows, but more by the vast amount of time I knew that the file represented.

I came to a file marked "Lustful Thoughts" and felt a chill run through my body. I pulled the file out only an inch, not wanting to test its size, and drew out a card. I shuddered at its detailed content. I felt sick to think that such a moment had been permanently recorded. Fear broke out in me. One thought dominated my mind: "No one, absolutely no one, must ever see these cards! No one must ever see this room! I must destroy it!"

In an insane frenzy, I yanked the whole file drawer out. Its size didn't matter now. I had to empty and burn the cards. But as I took it at one end and began pounding it on the floor, I could not dislodge a single card. I became desperate and pulled out a card only to find it as strong as steel when I tried to tear it. Defeated and utterly helpless, I returned the file to its slot. Leaning my forehead against the wall, I let out a long, self-pitying sigh.

Then the tears came and I began to weep. Sobs so deep that the hurt started in my stomach and shook through me. I fell on my knees and cried. I cried for shame, for the overwhelming shame of it all.

The rows of the file shelves swirled in my tear-filled eyes. No one must ever, ever know of this room. I must lock it up and hide the key. But then, as I pushed away the tears, I saw him. No, please, not him. Oh, anyone but Jesus! I watched helplessly as Jesus began to open the files and read the cards. I couldn't bear to watch his response. And in the moments I could bring myself to look at his face, I saw a sorrow deeper than my own. He seemed intuitively to go to the worst files. Why did he have to read every one? He turned and looked at me from across the room. He looked at me with pity in his eyes. But this was a pity that didn't anger me. I dropped my head, covered my face with my hands, and began to cry again. He walked over and put his arms around me. He could have said so many things. But he didn't say a word. He just cried with me.

Then Jesus got up and walked back to the wall of files. Starting at one end of the room, he took out a file, and, one by one, began to sign his name over mine on each card.

"*No!*" I shouted, rushing to him. All I could say was, "No! No!" as I pulled the card from him. His name shouldn't be on these cards, but there it was, written in red, so rich, so dark, so alive. The name of Jesus covered mine — it was written with his blood.

He gently took the card back. He smiled a sad smile and began to sign the cards. I don't think I'll ever understand how he did it so quickly, but the next instant it seemed I heard him close the last file and walk back to my side. He placed his hand on my shoulder, and whispered into my ear, "It is finished."

6. Preaching The Day Of Resurrection (Easter)

If the preacher's job for Good Friday is to get Jesus in the tomb, the preacher's job for Easter Day is to get him out.

My all-time favorite story to tell on Easter morning is the story of a large gathering in the old Soviet Union where a learned man spoke for an hour on the merits of atheism. When he was finished, a young Russian Orthodox priest asked if he could respond. The moderator said, "Yes, but you can only have five minutes." The priest replied, "I won't need that much time," and strode down the aisle, up to the platform, up to the microphone.

He looked out at the large crowed and shouted out in a loud voice, "Alleluia, Christ is Risen!" And the response thundered back, "The Lord is risen indeed, alleluia!"

49

The priest turned to the atheists on the platform and said, "That is my speech. I need no more time."[5]

I usually begin this story by practicing the Easter greeting and response and inviting them to respond wholeheartedly at the appropriate time in the story. If they don't do it with much gusto, I have them repeat it a few times until it gets up to a good shouting volume. Then I tell the story.

I think sometimes that if this story were the only thing I said on Easter morning, it would be sufficient.

One other observation that may guide your Easter Day sermon: Not all the Easter Day Gospel readings include an appearance of the risen Jesus. What if you preached the resurrection and had them come back the next Sunday (traditionally known as low Sunday) to hear the story of the actual risen Jesus?

7. Preaching Pentecost

It has been pointed out that this is the only major Christian feast day that has so far entirely escaped a commercial take-over. Apparently taking over Jesus' birth and his resurrection are one thing; messing with the Holy Spirit's day is another. Without any competition from the marketplace, go ahead and enjoy this unique opportunity, and preach your heart out on wind and fire.

----

1. Origin unknown.

2. Adapted from an article by the Reverend Brian Carsten, *"That strange and silly enterprise: Christianity,"* published in the newspaper of the Diocese of Northern Indiana, *The Beacon*, date unknown.

3. Wycliffe Bible Translators was a source of information.

4. Origin unknown, this story has appeared in numerous church newsletters and on the Internet, sometimes attributed to author Joshua Harris.

5. Origin unknown.

six

Preaching Special Occasions

1. Preaching At Weddings

Here is my favorite story to preach at weddings:[1]

A man went to an auction just to watch. But he noticed some of the vases that would be auctioned off, and he fell in love with one. So when the time came for the bidding, he put in his bid. The auctioneer bellowed out, "Going once, going twice ... you done bought it!"

The man took the vase home, and showed it off to everyone he could. But in the light of day, as he became more familiar with the vase, he could see its dents, nicks, and cracks. He took it back to the auctioneer to complain. The auctioneer refused to take it back. He said, "You bought it in 'as is' condition." The man who bought the vase looked at the auctioneer and said, "Then what am I supposed to do with it?" The auctioneer said to the man, "Sir, I suggest you love the hell out of it."

Marriage is like that. At first, you are just looking around. But you accidentally find each other and fall in love with each other. At the wedding, you commit yourselves to each other and take each other home. You show each other off. But sooner or later, you begin to see in the other person — dents, and nicks, and cracks. And you say, "Wait a second! I made a mistake! I want an exchange!" But you took each other in "as is" condition. And what are you supposed to do? I suggest you "love the hell" out of each other.

Using this story as an introduction, you can then go on to preach about what it means to love the hell out of each other, using your own sub-themes.

51

2. Preaching At Funerals[2]

There are four themes to capture in any funeral homily. First, a Christian understanding of grief as a normal, healthy process; second, gratitude for the life of the deceased; third, proclamation of the Word (the Christian faith rooted in the resurrection of Jesus Christ, as found in Holy Scripture), and fourth, an invitation to those present to grapple with the real questions of life and death. In other words, the homily helps the bereaved to consider in turn the deceased, the Redeemer Jesus Christ, and the living of their own lives.

I tend to take these up in the order given (I call them the four *G*s — grief, gratitude, God, and grappling). My reasoning for beginning with a few words on the grieving process is simply that the bereaved are typically very open to hearing about grief. It is not something that we talk about much in our society. For example, I usually say that people have many ways of grieving, that it's good to grieve, and then I encourage them to take the time needed to do it. This is a simple, pastoral way to begin the homily and invite people into it.

In time, mourners will experience the grief giving way to gratitude. It is helpful to encourage the bereaved to give thanks (and thereby begin that process, if it has not already begun). People are usually eager to do this, and it teaches thanksgiving as a very important part of our faith, in a way the bereaved can all embrace.

The third theme is the proclamation of the Word, using the main scripture or theological theme selected. I have a friend who calls this "preaching the comfort of Holy Scripture." I do not worry so much if it is comforting. I simply focus on preaching the Word, and leave whether it is comforting or challenging up to the hearer. Certainly the promise of eternal life to those who believe in Christ is comforting when the deceased professed and lived the faith. It may not be so comforting to others, and the Holy Spirit will have an opportunity to speak to hearts.

Lastly, it is always appropriate to invite the bereaved to see in this death an occasion to examine their own lives and grapple with the ultimate questions that get lost in everyday living. Death has brought us face-to-face again with the eternal questions. Let's ask them. A funeral homily may be the greatest opportunity to reach the lost that we regularly forfeit. When else do we have dozens, maybe even hundreds, of people listening to the Word who do not know Christ? They may not attend a worship service or hear a funeral homily again for months or years. We dare not forfeit that opportunity as ordained ministers and pastors who have promised to proclaim the gospel of Jesus Christ.

By addressing grief, gratitude, God, and inviting the bereaved to grapple with the meaning of their lives, we address those things the bereaved came to the funeral expecting, perhaps even eager to hear: something about the deceased, something about God and the Christian faith, and something about themselves. We will have used the funeral homiletic moment well!

3. Preaching At Installations Of New Pastors

If you are asked to preach at the installation of a new pastor, it is probably either because you are a good friend of the pastor, in which case the temptation might be to preach a sermon on how great your friend is, or, you are a friend of the congregation, in which case you might be tempted to preach on how great the congregation is. A good installation sermon will include a bit of both, but the main point to preach is the pastoral office in the context of parish ministry.

Since installations are festive occasions, humor is easily used and goes over well. Since the service can be extra long, like other special occasions, it is usually appropriate to use a short, to-the-point sermon.

---

1. Adapted from a sermon by The Reverend J. Gurdon Brewster, former chaplain, The Episcopal Church at Cornell University.

2. For funeral sermons based on the liturgical year, see Barbara G. Schmitz, *The Life of Christ and the Death of A Loved One: Crafting the Funeral Homily* (Lima, Ohio, CSS Publishing Company, Inc., 1995).

seven

The Final Amen

1. Where In Texas Are You From?

I have been preaching for some time now, and I usually get a fair amount of compliments after my sermons. I don't believe any of them. And I will tell you why. Before I was even ordained, I preached a sermon at Holy Trinity Episcopal Church in Lincoln, Nebraska. It was maybe the seventh sermon I had preached in my whole life. I thought it was pretty good at the time. Now that I am more experienced, let me be clear — it was not all that good. It wasn't bad for a seventh sermon, but it was far from a good sermon.

At the end of the service I stood in the back of the church to shake people's hands and greet them. A woman came up to me, introduced herself, and then introduced her sister who was visiting from Texas. The woman from Texas absolutely gushed over my sermon. She said it was the best sermon she had ever heard. It had deeply moved her. She wondered where I had learned to preach so well. And I beamed at such compliments.

After I had changed out of my vestments, I went to coffee hour, and naturally, I sought out this warm, wonderful, intelligent, witty, marvelous person from Texas. I spotted her, walked over to where she was standing with a coffee cup in her hand, and asked, "Where in Texas are you from?" She said, "What did you say?" So I said, "I just wondered what town you were from in Texas." Again she said, "What did you say?" So I asked again, starting to feel a bit of holy agitation, "Where in Texas are you from? My seminary roommate last year was from Texas, and I know Texas is a pretty big state, but I just wondered if maybe you knew each other, so, where are you from?"

At first she looked at me with a dumbfounded look. But I will give her credit. She looked me straight in the eyes, took a deep breath, and said, "I'm sorry, but I forgot both my hearing aids this morning, and I can't hear anything you are saying."

And that is why, when somebody says I preached a good sermon, I don't believe a word of it.

2. Beware Nodding Heads

I love it when I can see people responding to my sermon — smiling, nodding, laughing, saying, "Yes, that's happened to me too." I preached in a church where a young woman seemed to be tracking my sermon extraordinarily well, nodding her head, giving facial expressions of enlightenment and insight.

After the service, I met her at coffee hour. She was just as buoyant, her head bobbing up and down with delight. She said how much she appreciated my sermon. I thanked her and said I had noticed she seemed to really be into it. "Yes," she said, "I meant to tell you before the service, I am on some special medication, and I can't keep my head from nodding up and down."

3. "Nice Sermon"

Probably the most frequent comment I hear as people shake my hand and walk out of the church is, "Nice sermon." I generally take this as an insult. Unless it is from a dear old lady, "Nice sermon" translates into something like this: "You didn't really say anything I didn't already know, you didn't challenge me too much, it wasn't overly long, and besides, it was fairly pleasant to listen to your voice." But it is so much easier just to mumble, "Nice sermon," rather than to say all that in the time it takes to shake the preacher's hand.

I am pretty sure about this because a few years ago I started responding to "Nice sermon" by saying, "Oh, what did you like about it?" Big mistake. My question was met with silence, then embarrassment, then a hastily concocted answer. "Nice sermon" is also church language for "I fell asleep," or, "I really didn't follow anything you said but other people seemed to be getting it" or perhaps, "I spent the whole sermon time daydreaming about my roast in the oven."

Now that I'm wiser as to what "Nice sermon" means, it doesn't mean I've stopped asking, "What did you like about it?" But if I'm not in a provocative mood, I'll just respond, "Oh, I'm so glad you liked it," and leave it at that.

When I am preaching in more elite circumstances, such as large downtown churches or fine suburban churches, I will hear "lovely" sermon. It took me a while to figure out that "lovely" was just the upper crust, moneyed version of "I fell asleep...."

Occasionally I get a hearty, crisp "Good job" or "Good sermon" with the handshake. Mostly this comes from older men, and it feels like a bit of a job evaluation. It may mean anything from, "I didn't expect you to preach as well as you did," to "That was better than the usual fare we get around here," to "What you said was meaningful to me." I usually get the "Good sermon" response from people with more judging, evaluative mindsets. I'm pretty sure about this because (a) I'm a pretty judgmental kind of person, and (b) I say, "Good sermon," when the person preached better than I thought he or she was capable of doing.

Another confusing response, which holds a variety of possible meanings, is, "I hope you come back again." I generally take this to mean that, relatively speaking, I preached better than the last few folks who happened to preach at this church.

Which brings me to the preferred sermon responses. Certainly "Thank you" is appropriate and makes me feel that I said something helpful to someone. My typical response to "Thank you" is a simple, "You're welcome." Also ranking right up there in the nirvana of sermon responses is "That really spoke to me." Since this is what I pray happens every week, this response is most coveted.

So the only thing you really have to watch out for is the occasional person who raves over your sermon and says you're the greatest preacher on the face of the earth. I suggest you first check the person's ears and see if there is a hearing aid in there.

4. The Best Compliment Of All

But the best compliment of all is when someone asks you for a copy of the sermon. Of course, he could just be trying to flatter you, with no better intention than to dump that copy in the trash as soon as he gets home. But I believe most people, if not everybody who asks for a sermon, asks because something resonated deep within them and they want to have a reminder of it.

5. I've Heard All The Sermons

I preached fairly regularly at one church where a certain little old lady ("LOL" in clergy lingo) always came into the service just when I had finished preaching. Being an on-time kind of person myself, this rather irritated me but I didn't say anything to her about it.

One Sunday morning as she greeted me after the service, she looked up at me and asked, "Do you ever wonder why I come in right after the sermon?"

I looked at her and said, "As a matter of fact, yes, I do."

She said to me, "Well, I'm pretty old, as you can see, and I've heard all the sermons that there are, so I just skip that part and come in afterward."

Flabbergasted, I said nothing. However, if I ever have the chance again, I know what I will say. I will say something like this: "Honey, the Holy Spirit gave me this sermon last night at 2 a.m. in the morning. That sermon was hot off the press, and you missed it."

eight

Afterword

1. Everybody Only Has One Sermon

There is a saying among preachers that everybody has only one sermon. What they mean is that when it comes down to it, there's really only one fundamental truth deep in our guts and that's basically what we preach over and over, obviously with different slants and angles and stories from week to week, but it all boils down to this one thing.

I think for a lot of preachers that "one sermon" is "God is love" or "Amazing grace." For me, it is Romans 8:28: "All things work together for good for those who love God." That is the bass note you can hear in every one of my sermons.

It's not good or bad, here nor there, that we all have one sermon. It's just good to be aware of it, in case it's not the most helpful sermon — for example, some preachers' one sermon is "All have sinned" or "The world is full of evil" — both are true, but that's not a great basis for preaching week after week.

2. Preaching To Myself

There is another saying among preachers that scares me even more than the saying that we all have only one sermon: it is that when we are preaching, we are preaching to ourselves, or, another way I have heard it put, our best sermons are the ones we are actually preaching to ourselves.

After a decade of preaching, I believe it is true. When I have been betrayed and hurt, I can preach a great sermon on forgiveness. When I am in despair, I can preach a great sermon on hope. When I am grieving a loss, what a sermon I can preach on resurrection and new life! When I am grateful and feeling blessed, what a sermon I can preach on gratitude!

As I gather up the fragments of my everyday life to preach the Good News of the gospel, I may like to think that God is objectively using these gifts of writing and speech in some pure way to bring good news to hungry, thirsty people. Like Phillips Brooks, I expect to see repentance, conversion, and changed parishioners every time I preach. I have a holy expectation about what every sermon will accomplish in the lives of the hearers. But in the end, the real miracle of preaching is this: I really am preaching to myself, and somehow, God is able to use it to reach many people.